THE SUN & MOON SIGNS LIBRARY

JUNE 22 – JULY 22

JULIA AND DEREK PARKER

Photography by Monique le Luhandre

Illustrations by Danuta Mayer

DK

DORLING KINDERSLEY

London • New York • Stuttgart

Dedicated to Kenneth Styles

A DORLING KINDERSLEY BOOK

Editor **Tom Fraser**
Art Editor **Ursula Dawson**
Managing Editor **Krystyna Mayer**
Managing Art Editor **Derek Coombes**
Production **Antony Heller**
U.S. Editor **Laaren Brown**

Computer page make-up Patrizio Semproni.
Photography p 10 Ronald Sheridan/Ancient Art and Architecture Library;
p 11 ©Michael Holford/British Museum; p 16 Tim Ridley.
Stylist pp 28-29 Lucy Elworthy. Illustration pp 60-61 Kuo Kang Chen.
Jacket illustration Peter Lawman. With thanks to Carolyn
Lancaster and John Filbey.

First American Edition, 1992
10 9 8 7 6 5 4 3 2 1

Published in the United States by
Dorling Kindersley, Inc., 232 Madison Avenue
New York, N.Y. 10016

Published in Great Britain by Dorling Kindersley Limited. Distributed by
Houghton Mifflin Company, Boston.

Library of Congress Catalog Card Number 92-52787
ISBN 1-56458-087-3

Reproduced by GRB Editrice, Verona, Italy
Printed and bound in Hong Kong by Imago

CONTENTS

INTRODUCING CANCER

CANCER, THE SIGN OF THE CRAB, IS THE FOURTH SIGN OF THE ZODIAC. WHILE A CRAB CAN SOMETIMES BE CRABBY, CANCERIANS PROJECT MANY EXTREMELY POSITIVE QUALITIES THAT MIGHT BE ASSOCIATED WITH THIS CREATURE.

Similarly to the way in which a crab's hard shell protects a soft interior, Cancer's subjects develop a hard psychological shell to protect themselves and their loved ones from the rigors of life. If you challenge or threaten a Cancerian in any way, you will see this self-defensive system spring into action at once.

Traditional groupings

As you read through this book you will come across references to the elements and the qualities, and to positive and negative, or masculine and feminine signs.

The first of these groupings, that of the elements, comprises fire, earth, air, and water signs. The second, that of the qualities, divides the Zodiac into cardinal, fixed, and mutable signs. The final grouping is made up of positive and negative, or masculine and feminine signs. Each Zodiac sign is associated with a combination of components from these groupings, all of which contribute different characteristics to it.

Cancerian characteristics

Cancer is the first sign of the water element, and therefore has a very high emotional level and great intuition. Possessing an excellent memory, Cancerians sometimes recall minor injuries and slights best forgotten. As a sign of the cardinal quality, however, Cancer is outgoing toward loved ones, as well as being kind, helpful, and considerate.

The sign's ruling "planet" is the Moon. The changeability of the Moon is reflected in Cancerians: They are exceptionally prone to moodiness and sudden changes of outlook. Cancer is linked with silvery blue and smoky gray colors that reflect the colors of the Moon. It is a feminine, negative sign, which inclines its subjects toward introversion.

The Zodiac Wheel

The relationship between each Zodiac sign and the traditional astrological groupings is made clear within the Zodiac wheel. As you read through this book you will also discover references to polar, or opposite signs, and these, too, can be easily worked out by referring to the wheel.

CANCER
MYTHS & LEGENDS

THE ZODIAC, WHICH IS BELIEVED TO HAVE ORIGINATED IN BABYLON AS LONG AS 2,500 YEARS AGO, IS A CIRCLE OF CONSTELLATIONS THROUGH WHICH THE SUN MOVES DURING THE COURSE OF A YEAR.

The sign of Cancer probably originated in Ancient Egypt, where the constellation was first known as the sign of the Stars of the Water and later as the Two Turtles (river turtles are found in the Nile and have a hard shell, like that of a crab). In Ancient Babylon, the sign was known not only as Al. lul, a water creature – "the wicked or rebellious one" – but also as bulug, the Crab or Crayfish. Much later, the Ancient Greeks named it the Tortoise.

Hercules and the Hydra
In this fourth-century image the crab is seen assisting the Hydra.

The labors of Hercules

Of all the Zodiac signs, this constellation is perhaps the least celebrated in myth and legend. The only association that has really been made is with one of the 12 labors that the hero Hercules was made to perform by King Eurystheus, the ruler of Greece, after he had murdered his own wife and children. Having consulted the Oracle at Delphi, Hercules learned that only by showing obedience to Eurystheus could he atone for his crime. The second labor consisted of the destruction of the Hydra, a monster specially reared by the goddess Hera to fight him. It had the body of a dog, and nine snaky heads – one of which was immortal. Furthermore, its breath was so poisonous that anyone unfortunate enough to be exposed to it fell dead instantly. From its den in a marsh

near Lerna in the Peloponnese, it would embark on great orgies of destruction and killing, devastating innumerable herds and crops.

Hercules battles the Hydra

Hercules forced the Hydra to leave its marsh by showering the beast in flaming arrows. At first his task seemed impossible, every time he struck off one of the monster's heads, two more grew in its place. Moreover, when Hercules eventually seemed to be gaining an advantage in his battle with the Hydra, Hera sent a great crab to help out, which it did by attacking the hero's foot. In the end, however, Hercules succeeded in stamping on it, disposing of it for good. Nevertheless, Hera was so grateful for the crab's assistance that she set it among the stars in a constellation of its own, which we call Cancer. Hercules went on to kill the Hydra by burning off its mortal heads with a red-hot branding iron, before slicing off its immortal head.

The characteristics of a crab can often be seen in people associated with this sign. Cancerians usually have a brittle protective shell, evident in an exterior gruffness; but this shell usually conceals a caring personality.

Egyptian mummy and coffin

This ancient wooden coffin, dating from the second century A.D., is decorated with the signs of the Zodiac.

CANCER
SYMBOLISM

CERTAIN HERBS, SPICES, FLOWERS, TREES, GEMS, METALS, AND ANIMALS HAVE LONG BEEN ASSOCIATED WITH PARTICULAR ZODIAC SIGNS. SOME ASSOCIATIONS ARE SIMPLY AMUSING, WHILE OTHERS CAN BE USEFUL.

Flowers

Plants that flower at night are connected with Cancer. Other Cancerian flowers include acanthus, honeysuckle, and white flowers such as the white rose and lily.

WHITE LILIES

WHITE ROSES

LAUREL

Trees

Cancer is said to have a special sympathy for all trees. This association is particularly strong with those trees that are rich in sap.

Herbs

Saxifrage, which calms the stomach, and purslane, good for liver ailments, are both Cancerian herbs.

SAXIFRAGE

NUTMEG

Spices

No particular spice is associated with Cancer, but coriander and nutmeg are sometimes mentioned in connection with water signs.

CORIANDER

CANCER
SYMBOLISM

Animals

The crab is, of course, associated with this sign; but so are all animals with shells or tough hides, such as the tortoise, crocodile, and armadillo.

TORTOISESHELL COMB

TORTOISESHELL BOX

FAN WITH MOTHER-OF-PEARL STICKS

CRAB

Gems

The Cancerian gem is the pearl – its luster is closely associated with the Moon, which rules Cancer.

PEARL NECKLACE

LOCKET DECORATED WITH PEARLS

Metal

Silver is the Cancerian metal. Those born under this sign often like to wear silver jewelry.

SILVER FILIGREE SPOONS

ANTIQUE SILVER PICTURE FRAME

CANCER PROFILE

THE APPEARANCE OF TYPICAL CANCERIANS OFTEN REFLECTS THEIR HOARDING INSTINCTS. FAVORITE OLD JACKETS, OR SOME REFERENCE TO THE PAST, ARE USUALLY IN EVIDENCE. CARELESSNESS CAN SOMETIMES SPOIL THEIR IMAGE.

Many Cancerians fail to stand as straight as they should. They are often a little round-shouldered, which can tend to make them look rather fearful or apprehensive.

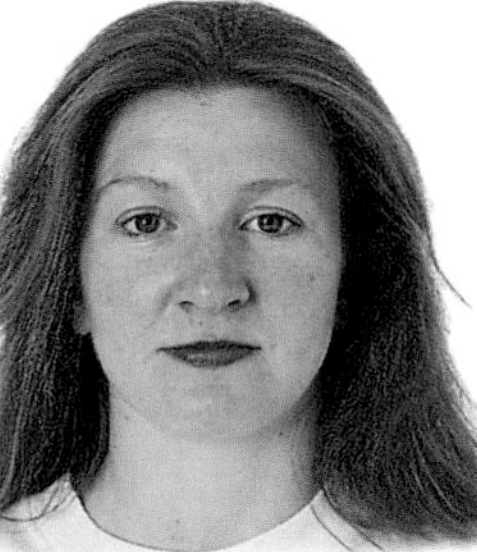

The Cancerian face
Long red hair, and a pale and sometimes sensitive complexion, are both typically Cancerian characteristics.

The body

Cancerians are generally good cooks. You may therefore tend toward being a little overweight if you are not careful about what you eat. Unless you are really keen on taking exercise you could be a little more prone to becoming flabby than many other Zodiac types.

You have a strong constitution, and will have excellent powers of resistance to illness. Many women of this sign have more than ample bosoms, which can be an asset to their powers of attraction.

The face

Cancerians often have rather long hair, which can become a little untidy if it does not receive the appropriate amount of care. Red hair is very common among Cancerians. Your forehead is likely to be rather pale and pronounced, perhaps with frown lines between the eyes. The eyes themselves are usually on the small side; some Cancerians may have rather beady little eyes. Even among races with dark skin coloring, Cancerians tend to have pale skin that is rather sensitive to the sun. It is possible that scar tissue will show on

The Cancerian stance

Many Cancerians tend to hunch themselves up when they stand; this can make them look rather apprehensive.

your skin long after a wound has healed. As a Cancerian, your mouth is likely to be soft and flexible.

Style

The Cancerian style is often very distinctive. A particularly smart image is often spoiled by choosing the wrong accessories or by sheer carelessness: you may for example sometimes leave a shoulderstrap showing, or wear an untidily knotted tie. Because of this tendency you need to take great care over the way you decide to dress – more, in fact, than members of any other sign. You could have a preference for antique clothes, which can be very attractive.

You are likely to have a very good sense of color. Soft shades of blue or gray often complement the Cancerian personality. Many Cancerians also choose the fabric for their clothes extremely skillfully.

In general

Your overall appearance may be marked by a tendency to stoop, and glance furtively around you to make sure that you are not about to be challenged. As a Cancerian, you are probably also likely to pay an unusual amount of attention to the weather. In your efforts to pre-empt and cater for every type of weather condition you may sometimes appear exaggeratedly swathed in heavy layers of warm clothes and thick scarves when it is cold, but also dress extremely lightly when it is hot.

CANCER

PERSONALITY

KINDNESS AND SENSITIVITY ARE DOMINANT FEATURES OF THE CANCERIAN PERSONALITY. WHILE THEY THEMSELVES ARE EASILY HURT, CANCERIANS ARE OFTEN UNAWARE THAT THEY CAN BE HARSH IN THEIR RESPONSES TO OTHERS.

The first time that someone meets you, it may be easy for them to get the wrong impression. This is because you can tend to act a little defensively toward people you do not know; you develop your own hard shell in order to protect yourself. Underneath this, however, you probably feel very vulnerable.

If others are tactful to you and take their time in getting to know you, it should not be too difficult for them to break through your defenses. When this happens, your deeply caring and understanding nature will shine through. Those who succeed in gaining your friendship will discover that you have the capacity to be a really good friend.

At work

You have a marvelously fertile imagination and should aim to use it positively and creatively under all circumstances. This applies to the way you approach your work. Only then will you be able to express your potential in the best possible way.

Your attitudes

You are probably the most tenacious of all Zodiac types, and you hang on tightly to your friends and loved ones. While you are tremendously faithful and want to do as much as possible for your family, it can be extremely difficult for you to accept the fact that your children will want to leave home and build their own lives once they grow up.

The overall picture

One of the most common character traits shared by all Cancerians, which is linked to your tenacity, is a strong tendency to hoard. You will hardly ever throw anything away – so much so that you and your home will inevitably become surrounded by clutter. If, however, you decide to

The Moon rules Cancer

The Moon, represented here by the goddess Diana, is usually shown as feminine. It encourages Cancerians to act instinctively, and influences the emotions and the digestive system.

take a serious interest either in antiques or in collecting articles that you find fascinating, this tendency will be put to good use.

By rechanneling your Cancerian hoarding instinct into a love of collecting things, you will be able to avoid having much of your space consumed by ugly heaps of newspapers, battered pots and pans, and any old junk – for example, pieces of string that are too short to be of any possible use to anyone.

Having said this, many Cancerians do have extremely good taste, and when this is fully developed, it really shows in every aspect of their lives. You are more than likely to have a great appreciation of, and sensitivity toward, everything that is beautiful.

CANCER
ASPIRATIONS

CARE-GIVING PROFESSIONS OFFER IDEAL WORK FOR CANCERIANS. YOU WILL PARTICULARLY ENJOY WORKING WITH YOUNG CHILDREN. AND SINCE YOU MAY BE THE BEST COOK IN THE ZODIAC, CATERING COULD ALSO APPEAL TO YOU.

Flight attendant
Working as a flight attendant or a courier involves a strong element of service, and you will therefore probably enjoy either profession.

MODEL JET

WHISK

SAUCEPAN

EGGS

Cooking
Cancerians are the natural cooks of the Zodiac. You may, however, be just a little temperamental when working with others in a kitchen.

QUILL PEN

Author

Many Cancerians are inspired by history and romance. You could be successful as a fiction writer in either of these areas.

1920S GLASS INKWELL

Caring professions

Caring for children may come naturally to you. You could find working in the social services particularly rewarding.

MERCURY THERMOMETER

BLOTTING PAPER

Teaching

You could well receive pleasure from inspiring young children and helping them to develop their minds. Your powerful imagination will be a great asset to you in this profession.

ABACUS

CANCER
HEALTH

THE PREVAILING ATMOSPHERE WILL HAVE A PHYSICAL, AS WELL AS AN EMOTIONAL, EFFECT ON A SENSITIVE CANCERIAN. YOUR RESPONSES TO THIS ATMOSPHERE ARE LIKELY TO BE HIGHLY INDIVIDUAL.

Sun sign Cancerians usually have somewhat pale complexions, irrespective of their background. This is not, however, a clue to how healthy or unhealthy they may be. In fact, you have a fairly strong constitution.

Your diet

As long as you beware of consuming too much cholesterol, you will benefit from a diet that includes a lot of dairy products. You may need to supplement your diet with calcium fluoride (calc. fluor.). This is considered to be important for the health of the teeth, fingernails, and bones.

Of all the 12 Zodiac signs, Cancerians are particularly prone to worrying. When you become upset, you may find yourself suffering from digestive problems.

Taking care

The traditional Cancerian body area is the breasts. Although this sign has no connection at all with breast cancer, it is sensible for all women to perform regular self-examinations. The sensitive Cancerian skin is a problem area. Protect yourself against the strong rays of the sun, as you are prone to sunburn.

Melon

Fruit and vegetables with a high water content, such as melons and pumpkins, are among the foods associated with Cancer.

Astrology and the body

For many centuries it was impossible to practice medicine without a knowledge of astrology. In European universities, medical training included information on how planetary positions would affect the administration of medicines, the bleeding of patients, and the right time to pick herbs and make potions. Each Zodiac sign rules a particular part of the body, and textbooks always included a drawing that illustrated the point.

CANCER AT LEISURE

EACH OF THE SUN SIGNS TRADITIONALLY SUGGESTS SPARE-TIME ACTIVITIES, HOBBIES, AND VACATION SPOTS. CONSIDER SOME OF THESE SUGGESTIONS – THEY OFTEN SUIT CANCERIAN INTERESTS.

POSTAGE STAMPS

Writing

Cancerians often have fertile imaginations, and these can be expressed through creative writing.

1920S FOUNTAIN PEN

Travel

Although a nervous traveler, you may enjoy a cruise. Your ideal location could be near a lake or the sea. Try Scotland, Holland, New Zealand, Paraguay, and North Africa as vacation destinations.

Cookery

It is typical for Cancerians of either sex to find cooking for their friends and family very fulfilling.

WOODEN SPOONS FOR COOKING

Sailor's shackle for securing rope

Silver perfume bottle

Sailing

Since Cancer is a water sign, many of its subjects are never happier than when enjoying themselves in boats. Some become skillful sailors.

Silverwork

Silver can be quite important to Cancerians, so much so that they often enjoy silverwork. It is the metal associated with the Moon, which rules Cancer.

Sewing

This is often a Cancerian hobby. Making children's clothes can be a particular specialty.

Toy sewing machine

Collection of shells and coral

Collecting

Cancerians are the hoarders of the Zodiac. If this tendency is directed toward forming an unusual collection of some kind, it can be most rewarding.

CANCER IN LOVE

MANY OF THE BEST CANCERIAN QUALITIES SPRING INTO ACTION WHEN CANCER FALLS IN LOVE. THOUGH YOU ARE ROMANTIC AND PASSIONATE, YOUR REACTIONS TO BOTH THE GOOD AND BAD THINGS IN A RELATIONSHIP CAN BE EXTREME.

While Cancerian emotions find a wonderfully positive outlet when you fall in love, it is also very easy for you to express certain traits that can have a negative effect on a relationship. If, however, you are conscious of the fact that you can create a more unpleasant atmosphere for your partners than you realize, you will be able to correct yourself before anything goes drastically wrong.

You have a very powerful motivation to love, cherish, and protect your loved ones. Unless you are careful, you may end up taking this tenderness too far and create a claustrophobic atmosphere within your relationship. Many people are unable to cope with this, finding it too confining, so this tendency to limit independence or freedom of expression may sometimes come between you and your lover.

As a lover

You are likely to take your love life very seriously, and while this does not mean that you do not enjoy – indeed revel in – love and sex, it does mean that due to a strong homemaking and family-raising instinct, you may tend to look upon all relationships with this in mind.

You should be aware that many prospective partners may not be so interested in a serious commitment. You are, no doubt, a wonderful lover, since you are both sensuous and in possession of a great instinct for the kind of things that are likely to make your partners happy.

Types of Cancerian lover

When Cancerians are young, it is a good idea for them to play the field. This way, they will gain experience with the opposite sex, and later, they are experienced and mature enough to cope with a stable, long-term relationship.

The influence of other planets will produce some subtle differences from one Cancerian to the next. Some of the more clinging members of the sign will be warmly affectionate as well as passionate, but can be very possessive. Others have a wonderfully flirtatious streak, which lightens their Cancerian intensity in love; yet another group has a lot of style and elegance, and will put partners on a pedestal. Some people of this Sun sign group display a sense of modesty that often intrigues prospective partners.

CANCER AT HOME

A CANCERIAN'S DWELLING PLACE IS, ABOVE ALL, A HOME. THE LOOK OF THE ROOMS USUALLY TAKES SECOND PLACE TO CONVENIENCE, WHICH IS OFTEN THAT OF THE CHILDREN. THIS CAN LEAD TO SUPREME UNTIDINESS.

When choosing a place to live you would do well to remember that Cancerians need a degree of peace and tranquility, perhaps in the form of a beautiful view, close at hand. This does not mean that you will feel unhappy living anywhere other than the heart of the country; a tiny balcony, or a corner filled with flowers, will provide you with a quiet, calming focus. The Cancerian home will ideally be quite close to a water source such as a slow-moving river, the sea, or a lake.

Wicker sewing basket
A sewing basket, knitting, or toys may be scattered around your home.

Furniture

Cancerians love the past, and hate to throw anything away. You are likely to choose either very traditional designs or, if you can afford it, quality antique furniture. You may become so fond of articles such as favorite armchairs that you will cling to them until they eventually begin to fall to pieces.

With well-developed Cancerian taste you may, however, choose quite beautiful, extremely comfortable furniture. Since your home is likely to be so important to you, the overall effect and atmosphere may be a joy to experience.

Soft furnishings

Cancerians look to the past when deciding on drapes. Your choice may veer either toward heavy silk brocades in pale silvery gray, or pastel colors, or alternatively Victorian chintz. When

Jug and fabric
These objects reflect the Cancerian colors and metal.

choosing new drapes, make sure that they are not too heavy, and try not to create a claustrophobic atmosphere. A Cancerian will have no desire to be overlooked by neighbors, but if you happen to live near the sea or a river, you will certainly want to see it clearly. If this is the case, drapes will definitely take a back seat.

Many Cancerians enjoy creating their own cushions, perhaps using petit point or some other form of decorative needlework.

Decorative objects

The tendency to hoard can ruin the effect of the Cancerian home. It may become extremely cluttered. If, however, your tendency to hoard can be controlled, and expressed through showing off an interesting personal collection of some kind, this will obviously enhance the overall appearance of your home.

You may choose to display a painting of your children, or perhaps a seascape. If you are fortunate enough to own some silver, or perhaps some family heirlooms, these are likely to be prominently displayed. Cancerians should accept the fact that sentimentality about old things can tend to be rather counterproductive.

Armchair and doll
A comfortable, well-worn armchair may be a much-loved item in your home.

THE
MOON
AND
YOU

THE SUN DECREES YOUR OUTWARD EXPRESSION, YOUR IMAGE, AND MANY IMPORTANT PERSONALITY TRAITS. THE MOON, ALTHOUGH MERELY THE EARTH'S SATELLITE, IS ASTRONOMICALLY THE SECOND MOST IMPORTANT BODY IN THE SOLAR SYSTEM. FROM THE SIGN THAT IT WAS IN AT YOUR BIRTH, IT INFLUENCES HOW YOU REACT TO SITUATIONS, YOUR EMOTIONAL LEVEL, AND, TO A CERTAIN EXTENT, WHAT YOU HAVE INHERITED FROM YOUR PARENTS AND ANCESTORS. HAVING FOUND YOUR MOON SIGN IN THE SIMPLE TABLES ON PAGES 56 TO 59, TURN TO THE RELEVANT PAGES AND TAKE A STEP FORWARD IN YOUR OWN SELF-KNOWLEDGE.

THE MOON IN ARIES

JUST AS CANCER IS THE FIRST WATER SIGN, SO ARIES IS THE FIRST FIRE SIGN. BOTH SIGNS HAVE HIGH EMOTIONAL LEVELS. YOUR ARIEN MOON ADDS ENTHUSIASM TO YOUR CHARACTER, WHICH YOU ARE LIKELY TO EXPRESS AT A MOMENT'S NOTICE.

You will be eager to surge ahead with projects and to accept challenges. Cancerians are noted for being both brave and protective, and these qualities are strongly emphasized in your personality.

Self-expression

In some respects a combination of fire and water elements is not an easy one. But your fire sign Moon works positively: you will be far less apprehensive, and less introverted, than some Cancerians.

You are one of the tougher types of Cancerian and will be able to cope extremely well during demanding and strenuous periods. Perhaps your instinctively adventurous spirit will encourage you to be something of an explorer, with a penchant for visiting unusual places.

Cancerian moods, spiced with sudden emotional flare-ups, could make you a force to be reckoned with. You should try to control these impulsive outbursts; they might be more potent than you realize.

Romance

You are extremely passionate, and it is in your love life that your very high emotional level will be best expressed. However, while your Cancerian Sun makes you somewhat clinging, your Arien Moon dictates that you need an element of independence and freedom.

Your well-being

The Arien body area is the head: If you are worried, you may tend to get unpleasant headaches. These may also be due to slight kidney upsets.

Planning ahead

As well as having plenty of Cancerian shrewdness and a good business sense, you react extremely well to enterprising schemes and suggestions.

The Moon in Aries

You should, however, always think carefully before becoming involved in them, in order to avoid disappointment later.

Parenthood

A great sense of fun and a marked sentimental streak color your attitude to life – this will certainly rub off on your loved ones. Like all Cancerians, you will be eager to have children, but you will be less prone to worry about them than most people of your Sun sign. But make sure that you recognize the fact that, in due course, they will want to move away from home and live their own lives. Your Aries Moon should help you to understand this and to ensure that you do not feel life is too empty once they are gone. Try to always look to the future and to see life through your children's eyes; otherwise, your Cancerian nostalgia and sentimentality could create a generation gap.

THE MOON IN TAURUS

AS AN EARTH SIGN, YOUR TAUREAN MOON WILL STABILIZE YOUR CANCERIAN QUALITIES AND ADD A PRACTICAL INSTINCT, AS WELL AS AN APTITUDE FOR MAKING MONEY. BEWARE OF ACTING TOO POSSESSIVELY TOWARD LOVED ONES.

Earth and water signs complement each other well, and while the Moon, which rules Cancer, exerts a very powerful influence over all Cancerians it is, by tradition, well placed in Taurus. As a result you will share many of the qualities commonly attributed to Taurus.

Self-expression

It is extremely important for you to feel both materially and emotionally secure. Provided you can do this, you will flourish and be able to express many fine positive qualities.

Through Taurus, you are warm and affectionate, and will not find it difficult to combine these traits with your caring, protective Cancerian traits. But you must ensure that possessiveness, which is the worst Taurean fault, does not obscure your warmth and kindness. On another level, your Cancerian instinct toward hoarding things, together with your instinctive love of possessions, will make it difficult for you to throw anything away.

Romance

You have the capacity to love both deeply and very passionately. Cancerians are noted for the sensual expression of their emotions, and when this is combined with the warm passion of a Taurean Moon, your partners may consider themselves very fortunate indeed. You have the ability to make and maintain a long-lasting relationship.

Your well-being

The Taurean body area is the throat, so yours could be vulnerable. More importantly, if you happen to be one of those great Cancerian cooks, the likelihood is that you will specialize in making very rich desserts with lots of cream, chocolate, and liqueurs. Many Cancerians tend to put on weight

The Moon in Taurus

easily, and Taurean good looks are often endangered by their fondness for good food. In short, be careful. If you have a slow metabolism, try to speed it up a little by getting some sensible exercise.

Planning ahead

Cancerian shrewdness combines extremely well with the Taurean ability to make money. You have very valid instincts in this area. There should be no problems when you have money to invest. In fact, if you discuss your finances with professional advisers, you could end up advising them.

Parenthood

Given the Cancerian tendency to cling, and Taurean possessiveness, you should be constantly aware of the problems that can arise when you are bringing up children. Still, you have the potential to be a wonderful parent. You will be sensitive to your children's needs, giving them much love and affection.

THE MOON IN GEMINI

YOU ARE PROBABLY ABLE TO COME UP WITH PERTINENT AND WITTY COMMENTS WITH VERY LITTLE EFFORT. GEMINIAN LOGIC COMES IN HANDY WHEN YOUR CANCERIAN IMAGINATION GETS THE BETTER OF YOU.

The elements – Cancer is a water sign and Gemini, air – add a variety of interesting facets to your personality. You are quick to respond to situations and are able to act rationally under stress. Your Cancerian tendency to worry will probably be filtered by an ability to look at problems very objectively.

A powerful Cancerian trait is moodiness. Here, however, your Geminian Moon helps to steady you; it will influence your reactions and create a balance.

Self-expression

Cancerians usually have very powerful imaginations, but sometimes this potential is not quite as well developed as it should be. Your Geminian Moon will help, since it will intellectualize this area. You may have an ability for storytelling or writing, or for using your hands creatively in craftwork of all kinds. Geminians can be restless and inconsistent. Always make sure that you go on to complete every project that you begin, and counter any restlessness and inconsistency in your personality.

Romance

You may not be quite as easily overwhelmed by emotion as many people of your Sun sign. Like all of them, however, you are a genuinely caring and protective lover.

It is also very important for you to have a good tie of friendship within your relationship and to share common interests with your partner. You should consider this very carefully before deciding to deepen an emotional relationship.

Your well-being

The Geminian body area covers the arms and hands; if you are a Cancerian cook or work with metals or tools, these may be especially vulnerable.

The Moon in Gemini

The Geminian organ is the lungs. Any time you get a cold that settles in your chest, seek medical advice as soon as possible.

Planning ahead

Although you will probably possess Cancerian shrewdness and instinctively sound business sense, you may be attracted to get-rich-quick schemes. If this is the case, be wary of your initial reactions; they could let you down. Always take your time when making decisions of this kind. You may have the ability to sell and will get a good price for anything you can bring yourself to part with. Cancerians are collectors and you may be attracted to gadgets of some kind, such as animated toys.

Parenthood

You are more modern in outlook, more logical, and far less clinging than most other Cancerian parents. Being less sentimental and nostalgic than many Cancerians, the generation gap should not be a problem for you.

THE MOON IN CANCER

WITH BOTH THE SUN AND THE MOON IN CANCER ON THE DAY OF YOUR BIRTH, YOU WERE BORN UNDER A NEW MOON, AND ARE KNOWN AS A DOUBLE CANCER. SINCE THE MOON RULES CANCER, YOU MAY BE VERY CANCERIAN INDEED.

Reading a list of the characteristics of your sensitive, caring Sun sign, you will probably recognize that a great many of them apply to you. On average, out of a list of 20 personality traits of any particular Sun sign, most people will identify with 11 or 12. Because the Moon was also in Cancer when you were born, for you the average increases considerably.

Self-expression

Your Sun sign makes you caring; you will like to cherish and look after people. Your Moon sign accentuates this primary motivation. You will tend to be both moody and changeable, and it is necessary that you recognize these tendencies.

It is also important for you to realize that, like the crab which is the symbol of your sign, you can easily become rather "crabby," expressing your feelings in a remarkably terse, sharp, and hurtful way.

You should find some way of positively expressing your powerful emotions. It is an excellent idea for you to have at least one compelling interest aside from your career or home and family.

Romance

You have a great deal of love to give to your partner; this is probably the most important area of emotional expression for you. But it may well be that your imagination will need to find expression. It can make you a stunning lover, capable of giving great pleasure to your partners, but it could mean that you will always be worried about them. You may find yourself either becoming jealous or thinking that the worst has happened to them.

Your well-being

As far as your health is concerned, if you read pages 22 to 23 you will probably agree that you suffer from

The Moon in Cancer

most Cancerian ailments. Many of these relate to the tendencies to worry that have been described here.

Planning ahead

You will often read that Cancerians are very shrewd in business. Because both your Sun and your Moon signs are in Cancer, you rightly conclude that you would be wise to follow your instincts in this area.

Even more than many people, you like to feel the security of a healthy bank balance, although Cancerians sometimes tend to be a little tightfisted when it comes to actually spending their money. You probably know that Cancerians are the collectors (and also the hoarders!) of the Zodiac. Any unusual articles that you care to collect may well become valuable assets in the long term.

Parenthood

You will be eager to have children and should make an excellent parent. Recognize that your children are individuals who will want to create their own lifestyles and eventually start families. If you avoid being sentimental and nostalgic, the generation gap will not be a problem.

THE MOON IN LEO

CANCER AND LEO ARE NEIGHBORING ZODIAC SIGNS AND OFFER THEIR SUBJECTS CONTRASTING CHARACTERISTICS. IF YOU HAVE AN INSTINCTIVE URGE TO BE CREATIVE, DO NOT LET ANYONE, INCLUDING YOURSELF, CRAMP YOUR STYLE.

Your Cancerian caution contrasts vividly with the nature of your Leo Moon, which is a fire sign. You will therefore respond to most things with greater enthusiasm than many Sun sign Cancerians, and you will be less apprehensive, not so prone to worry, and much better organized.

Self-expression

The Cancerian tendency toward untidiness will be considerably mitigated by your Leo Moon; it gives you a certain style and elegance that many Cancerians lack. Leo creativity blends well with the Cancerian instinct for imaginative design, and finding some form of creative expression could be of great importance to you.

The worst Leo fault is bossiness. If you are accused of this, take heed. You respond extremely quickly to other people's remarks and actions, and when this trait is combined with the Cancerian tendency to be critically aggressive, you will see how, for you, sparks might occasionally fly.

Romance

Your Leo Moon gives you very warm and passionate emotions that will be beautifully expressed toward your loved ones. Sexually, you are probably quite assertive, and perhaps more willing to take the lead than many other Sun sign Cancerians.

Because Cancerians are sensitive, you could easily be hurt if difficulties arise within a relationship. In spite of the fact that your Leo Moon makes you brave and assertive in this area, when hurt you will creep into your Cancerian shell and lick your wounds.

Your well-being

The Leo body area is the spine, and you really need to indulge in a little exercise to keep it in good condition. If you have a sedentary job, make

The Moon in Leo

sure you have a good chair that supports your spine properly.

The Leo organ is the heart: if you follow the suggestions for exercising your spine, you will automatically be strengthening your heart, too.

Planning ahead

It is very likely that, although you have a shrewd Cancerian business sense, you will enjoy luxury and real quality more than many people of your Sun sign. In order to keep your Cancerian conscience happy, it might be wise to consider quality when you go shopping – that way you will get more value for your money and thoroughly enjoy what you may consider to be slightly extravagant. Do not be afraid to think big where investment is concerned.

Parenthood

You will be a very active, positive, and encouraging parent. If you keep the negative side of your imagination under control, you will not worry unduly about your children. Try to avoid any stubborn or dogmatic reactions to their ideas and suggestions, and you will also avoid the development of a generation gap.

THE MOON IN VIRGO

CANCER AND VIRGO ARE THE TWO ZODIAC SIGNS MOST PRONE TO WORRY. CANCERIAN WORRY IS INTUITIVE AND IMAGINATIVE; VIRGOAN, MORE INTELLECTUALLY ORIENTED. TRY TO BALANCE ONE WITH THE OTHER.

Your Sun sign is of the water element, and Virgo is of the earth element. Since water and earth are complementary elements, the influences of your Sun and Moon signs generally work well together.

Self-expression

Cancer and Virgo certainly share some positive common attributes, but the signs also vie with each other to be the worst worriers of the Zodiac. Cancerian worry is emotional; Virgoan worry is illogical. But Cancerians are cautious, and Virgoans are practical. These traits will help to counter the difficulty. Try to be more logical, and bolster this with Cancerian caution.

Romance

Your Cancerian emotions may be slightly inhibited when you need to express your feelings toward lovers. Virgoans are very modest, and when someone declares their affection for you, your immediate reaction may well be to recoil a little. Try to recognize the tendency, because it could limit your delightfully sensitive, sensual, and caring qualities.

You will tend to be very critical of your partners and may nag them. If you are accused of this, take heed.

Your well-being

The Virgoan body area is the stomach; your digestive system is related to your Cancerian Sun. As a result worrying can upset your stomach. Virgoans are also prone to nervous tension and stress, which can lead to migraines. Try to develop a sense of inner calm. Perhaps a relaxation technique such as yoga will be of help to you.

Planning ahead

Your Cancerian Sun sign makes you careful with money; your Virgoan Moon sign makes you even more

The Moon in Virgo

cautious. You therefore have the ability to save wisely. Just be sure to remember to enjoy the fruits of your labors. When investing, look for slow, steady growth.

Parenthood

Although Cancerians generally make warm, caring, and protective parents, you may tend to criticize your children a little too easily. This can be far more damaging than you might realize, especially if you have energetic, exuberant children. If you criticize them too much, they will probably lose their self-confidence In the long term, this could lead to problems, so guard against it.

Your creative imagination will stand you in good stead with your children. You are less likely than most people to have difficulty with the generation gap, since you will keep a keen and attentive eye on the values and opinions of the younger generation, encouraging lively discussions.

THE MOON IN LIBRA

IF YOUR INSTINCT TELLS YOU TO SWITCH OFF, CALM DOWN AND RELAX. BY FOLLOWING THAT INSTINCT, YOU WILL MAKE THE MOST OF YOUR FINE, DIPLOMATIC MOON IN LIBRA, AND KEEP YOURSELF IN BALANCE.

The cardinal quality is shared by both Cancer and Libra , and this gives you some very interesting personality traits.

Self-expression

No matter how busy you may be, the chances are that you will always have time for others. As a result, you may give the impression that you spend most of your time doing nothing. That is not, of course, the case. You will work hard to achieve whatever you set out to do.

You are diplomatic, and probably less likely than most Cancerians to give in to moodiness. You also have a natural instinct for beautiful things, and will want your environment and personal appearance to be pleasing.

Romance

A natural indecisiveness may make committing yourself more difficult for you than for many people. Once that commitment has been made, however, your Cancerian need for home and family life will be satisfied, and you will become a wonderful, loving partner.

You have a strong inclination toward romance, and this does a great deal to enhance both your love and sex lives. There is an air of calm and serenity about you – but this will not inhibit passionate Cancerian emotion.

Your well-being

The Libran organ is the kidneys. Recurrent headaches could indicate that you have a minor kidney disorder. On the other hand, headaches could also be the result of the Cancerian tendency to worry. Your Libran Moon will work in your favor in this area, telling you to calm down, switch off, and relax.

Bearing in mind that you could well love gourmet cooking and delicious food, and remembering that Librans

The Moon in Libra

often have a sweet tooth, there is obviously a danger that you may put on weight easily. Attend regular exercise classes at a large and friendly health club where there is the possibility of socializing after class.

Planning ahead

Cancerian financial caution could dampen a luxurious, pleasure-loving instinct bestowed on you by your Libran Moon. Look at it this way: You are clever with money, and have no lack of shrewdness, so why not give in to your love of luxury? It will make life fun and far more enjoyable, and will certainly help you relax.

Parenthood

You will probably have a more relaxed attitude about parenthood than many other Sun sign Cancerians, but you should be very careful that you do not confuse your children by being indecisive. You will always be happy to listen to your children, so in that respect there should be no difficulty with the generation gap.

THE MOON IN SCORPIO

CANCER AND SCORPIO ARE BOTH SIGNS OF THE WATER ELEMENT. YOUR MOON GIVES YOU A TERRIFIC SOURCE OF EMOTIONAL ENERGY; CHANNEL THIS WISELY, AND DO NOT RESORT TO BEING JEALOUS OR VINDICTIVE.

Because both Cancer and Scorpio are water signs, you are likely to have tremendous resources of emotional and physical energy. You must find fulfilling ways of expressing these, because inner satisfaction and psychological wholeness are of above-average importance to you.

Self-expression

Your work must satisfy you. If its demands are not enough for you and your lifestyle is equally unengaging, then develop a compelling spare-time interest. This should consume either your emotional or physical energy – or ideally, both. Cancerian tenacity and your urge to get to the bottom of every problem will blend well, whatever you do.

Romance

You have a great deal to contribute to a long-term relationship. As an extremely passionate lover, you can, however, be very demanding both sexually and in more general matters. You need an understanding partner, who is as eager as you are to live an active and full life. Should any Cancerian moods catch up with you, your partner will have to be considerate enough to understand.

The worst Scorpio fault is jealousy. If you allow your Cancerian imagination to work overtime, you could build up the most terrible tension in a relationship. Try to accept rational explanations and recognize that logic can escape you.

Your well-being

The Scorpio body area is the genitals, so regular health checks of this area are most advisable. You could be more prone to worry than is usual for Cancerians, and this could also have an effect upon your health. Remember, too, that a boring job will leave you lacking inner satisfaction.

The Moon in Scorpio

Planning ahead

You may have a really good business sense and perhaps a desire to set up and develop your own company. You are shrewd; your Cancerian Sun sees to that. But your Scorpio Moon will also stand you in excellent stead here.

Parenthood

Your Cancerian Sun makes you a good, but demanding, parent – it could be that you are considerably stricter than you may realize. You will be eager to spur your children into action, but be careful not to be too dogmatic. Encourage them, but remember that finding the appropriate kind of encouragement for each child may be difficult. Try not to push your children into following in your footsteps; they may find their own paths more rewarding. If you allow them the freedom of expression that is so necessary to young people, you will avoid problems with the generation gap.

THE MOON IN SAGITTARIUS

YOUR SAGITTARIAN INSTINCT IS FOR FREEDOM OF EXPRESSION AND INDEPENDENCE, BUT YOU ALSO VALUE CANCERIAN EMOTIONAL SECURITY AND YOUR FAMILY. LEARN TO COMPROMISE WHILE RETAINING YOUR OWN VALUES.

The combination of a Cancerian Sun and a Sagittarian Moon gives your personality some contrasting and very unusual aspects. It may even be that when you read descriptions of your Sun sign, you think some of the statements hold little or no truth at all for you.

Self-expression

You are likely to have a wider-ranging mind than other Sun sign Cancerians, incorporating qualities that differ from those normally associated with your Sun sign. While, for instance, you love and need the security of your home and family, claustrophobic feelings – brought on either by the physical layout of your home, or more psychologically, because of the pressures of family life – are something that you cannot cope with. It is important that you respond freely to the outgoing, extrovert levels of your personality. Do not let Cancerian sensitivity or inhibition cramp the open expressiveness of your Moon sign qualities.

Romance

Your attitude toward love is very positive. You will like to have fun and enjoy your relationships. Sagittarius is an emotional sign, and as a result you have abundant resources of outgoing emotion and passion.

It may be that you will take longer than many people of your Sun sign to settle into a permanent relationship. Before you do so, remember that you really need an intelligent partner, who will be equipped to stretch your mind.

Your well-being

The Sagittarian body area covers the hips and thighs. If you are a female Cancerian cook or simply love good food, you will tend to put on weight very easily around these areas. Male Cancerians can, all too easily, develop

The Moon in Sagittarius

paunches. Fortunately, you probably love many sports and participate in several. If this is not the case, try some kind of freely expressive dance. In complete contrast, horse-riding may appeal to you.

Planning ahead

A tendency to take risks can make you a little foolhardy when dealing with money. Remember, however, that Cancerians are usually shrewd and clever both in business and when dealing with cash. Try, therefore, to get the best of both your Sun sign and your Moon sign, and learn to enjoy the challenge of making money grow without letting a deep-rooted gambling instinct overpower you.

Parenthood

You will have a very positive attitude toward your children and, unlike many Cancerians, will probably not worry if they are a few minutes late getting home from school. You can inspire them, and if you allow an instinctive and very natural sense of enthusiasm full rein, you will gain their love and respect. You should have few problems with the generation gap.

THE MOON IN CAPRICORN

CANCER AND CAPRICORN ARE OPPOSITE OR POLAR ZODIAC SIGNS, SO YOU WERE BORN UNDER A FULL MOON. YOU ARE INHERENTLY PRONE TO RESTLESSNESS AND AN INNER DISCONTENT; TRY TO COUNTER ANY TENDENCY TO COMPLAIN.

You will probably be more ambitious, and aspire to greater achievements, than other Sun sign Cancerians. But because Capricorn is not particularly emotionally oriented, it may be that this ambition, which is usually so strong, will remain subdued. It is important that you do not suppress it.

Self-expression

Both Cancer and Capricorn are of the cardinal quality, and as a result, you possess the ability to use your energies freely and willingly for the benefit of others. For yourself, you have the capacity to achieve great pinnacles of happiness both at home and at work.

Be careful of one thing: You may have a tendency to grumble, especially when presented with challenges or suggestions that do not precisely fit in with your plans. This will not make you popular with other people. Be aware, too, that because you were born under a Full Moon you could tend to suffer from restlessness.

Romance

While Cancerian warmth and tenderness will color your attitude toward your partners, your first reaction when approached by a prospective lover could be slightly cool. They may well have to break through that initial chilliness, and perhaps get past the self-defensive Cancerian protective shell that could easily manifest itself if you begin to feel vulnerable or insecure. But your lover, having gained your confidence, does have someone very special, and you are more than likely to remain faithful forever.

Your well-being

The Capricornian body areas are the shins and knees. These, and your joints in general, are prone to stiffness

The Moon in Capricorn

and rheumatic pain. It is vital for you to find a form of exercise that will help you to keep mobile.

Planning ahead

One way in which the Cancerian and Capricornian "polarity" emerges is through the fact that both signs are known to be very careful with money. A little more generosity may create a more enjoyable lifestyle for you.

Your Capricornian Moon gives you a natural inclination and taste for real quality. You like to buy things that will really last – partly because you hate waste and probably loathe throwing things away. You will invest very wisely and, in general, will always aim for steady growth.

Parenthood

Avoid the tendency to distance yourself from your children. Make sure that you have fun, and that the quirky sense of humor which comes from your Capricornian Moon finds plenty of expression. By doing so, you will bridge the generation gap.

THE MOON IN AQUARIUS

TRY NOT TO BE AFRAID OF EXPRESSING YOUR UNCONVENTIONAL ORIGINALITY: IT OFFERS YOU THE CHANCE TO FIND CONSIDERABLE INNER SATISFACTION AND FULFILLMENT. AVOID DISTANCING YOURSELF FROM OTHERS.

Your air sign Aquarian Moon and water sign Cancerian Sun are not the best of bedfellows. You will, however, have some extremely interesting and unusual qualities that make you a truly fascinating person.

Self-expression

Your reactions to situations are somewhat unpredictable. On some occasions you can be sympathetic, but on others, shocked. Your Cancerian kindness and sensitivity are, however, complemented by some very humanitarian qualities. You will give both time and energy, as well as money, when and where you come across need – it will be this sense of need that instinctively motivates you. Having taken action, you will freely express your caring, protective Cancerian spirit.

Your Cancerian emotions are somewhat cooled by your Moon sign influences. You are able to rationalize your feelings and, if it becomes necessary, should be able to distance yourself from them.

Romance

At heart, you are very romantic, but it could be that an inner need for independence clashes with a desire to have your own home and family. You may be attracted to a lifestyle that is individual in some way.

A love of romance is never too far from the surface, and because of it, you are likely to enjoy love and sex in a romantic atmosphere. It should not be difficult for you to persuade your partner to go along with this. Since you have an intriguing air of glamour, and are attractive to the opposite sex, you should enjoy yourself.

Your well-being

The Aquarian body area is the ankles, and these are very vulnerable. The circulation is also governed by

The Moon in Aquarius

Aquarius, so you must be careful to take care of yourself when the weather is cold.

Planning ahead

Of all the Cancerian Sun and Moon sign combinations, yours may be the least practical when it comes to money. Of course, you have Cancerian shrewdness and business sense lurking somewhere in your personality, and you may be wasting your potential. Can you see yourself owning your own business? If you do, remember that you do not lack originality, and stand an excellent chance of finding a gap in the market.

Parenthood

As a parent, your tendency to be unpredictable, plus Cancerian changes of mood, may cause difficulties. Keeping abreast of your children's ideas and concerns will help you to come to terms with any generation gap problems.

THE MOON IN PISCES

A TENDER AND LOVING CANCERIAN, WITH THE POWERFUL FORCE OF PISCES, HAS A TORRENT OF EMOTIONAL ENERGY. USE THAT ENERGY AND NEVER UNDERESTIMATE YOURSELF OR YOUR ABILITIES.

While the combination of two water signs will serve to integrate your instincts and self-expression successfully, you should be careful that you are not entirely swayed by your reactions to people and by the power of your emotions.

Self-expression

You will automatically follow your intuition and natural instincts. Remember, though, that because you are so very kind, helpful, and charitable, and always ready to part with time, energy, and cash, people could take advantage of you all too easily. You may consciously have to develop your protective Cancerian shell, and at times you will have to be very firm with yourself if you wish to have complete control over your life.

Your Cancerian Sun gives you inner strength and tenacity, but a very tender and ultrasensitive Piscean Moon could sometimes tend to undermine your more powerful characteristics, especially when you are moved in some way.

Romance

If you get caught up with a partner who does not allow you the freedom to develop your potential and use your vivid imagination, think again.

You need a strong partner who will encourage you in all your efforts and take some of the strain, should an area of your life fall under pressure. There is a romantic, almost poetic, side to you, which colors your expression of love and sex – your partners should really enjoy it. Be careful that you do not delude yourself when you are in love, seeing every partner as your ideal, and try not to be deceptive.

Your well-being

The Piscean body area is the feet. These could cause you a lot of trouble. On the other hand, as can be

The Moon in Pisces

the case with astrology, the reverse could be true, and your feet may be healthy and problem-free.

The Cancerian tendency to worry will certainly affect you. Make sure that this does not become irrational and that your very powerful imagination does not take over. Be guided by your intuition and control any exaggerated reactions.

Planning ahead

Your Piscean Moon may overcome your practical, cautious Cancerian qualities when it comes to dealing with money. If you are aware of this, then perhaps, over a period of time, you will learn not to be a financial soft touch. Take advice from your financial consultant, accountant, or some other professional.

Parenthood

Children are bright and, from an early age, yours may know how to handle you. It may be necessary for you to act strictly from time to time.

Try not to be too clinging and sentimental, and remember that if you do not keep up with your children's way of thinking, you may have generation gap problems.

CANCER

MOON CHARTS

THE FOLLOWING TABLES WILL ENABLE YOU TO DISCOVER YOUR MOON SIGN. THEN, BY REFERRING TO THE PRECEDING PAGES, YOU WILL BE ABLE TO INVESTIGATE ITS QUALITIES, AND SEE HOW THEY WORK WITH YOUR SUN SIGN.

By referring to the charts on pages 57, 58 and 59 locate the Zodiacal glyph for the month of the year in which you were born. Using the Moon table on this page, find the number opposite the day you were born that month. Then, starting from the glyph you found first, count off that number using the list of Zodiacal glyphs (below, right). You may have to count to Pisces and continue with Aries. For example, if you were born on May 21, 1991, first you need to find the Moon sign on the chart on page 59. Look down the chart to May; the glyph is Sagittarius (♐). Then consult the Moon table for the 21st. It tells you to add nine glyphs. Starting from Sagittarius, count down nine, and you find your Moon sign is Virgo (♍).

MOON TABLE

DAYS OF THE MONTH AND NUMBER OF SIGNS THAT SHOULD BE ADDED

DAY	ADD	DAY	ADD	DAY	ADD	DAY	ADD
1	0	9	4	17	7	25	11
2	1	10	4	18	8	26	11
3	1	11	5	19	8	27	12
4	1	12	5	20	9	28	12
5	2	13	5	21	9	29	1
6	2	14	6	22	10	30	1
7	3	15	6	23	10	31	2
8	3	16	7	24	10		

ZODIACAL GLYPHS

♈	Aries
♉	Taurus
♊	Gemini
♋	Cancer
♌	Leo
♍	Virgo
♎	Libra
♏	Scorpio
♐	Sagittarius
♑	Capricorn
♒	Aquarius
♓	Pisces

	1923	1924	1925	1926	1927	1928	1929	1930	1931	1932	1933	1934	1935
JAN	♊	♏	♈	♌	♐	♈	♍	♑	♉	♎	♓	♋	♏
FEB	♌	♐	♉	♍	♑	♊	♏	♓	♋	♐	♈	♌	♑
MAR	♌	♑	♉	♍	♒	♋	♏	♓	♋	♐	♉	♍	♑
APR	♎	♓	♋	♏	♈	♍	♑	♉	♍	♒	♊	♎	♓
MAY	♏	♈	♌	♐	♉	♎	♒	♊	♎	♓	♋	♐	♈
JUN	♑	♉	♍	♒	♋	♏	♓	♌	♐	♉	♍	♑	♊
JUL	♒	♋	♏	♓	♌	♐	♈	♍	♑	♊	♎	♓	♋
AUG	♈	♌	♐	♉	♍	♒	♊	♏	♓	♋	♐	♈	♌
SEP	♉	♎	♒	♋	♏	♓	♌	♐	♈	♍	♑	♊	♎
OCT	♊	♏	♓	♌	♐	♉	♍	♑	♉	♎	♓	♋	♏
NOV	♌	♑	♉	♍	♑	♊	♏	♓	♋	♐	♈	♌	♑
DEC	♍	♒	♊	♎	♓	♌	♐	♈	♌	♑	♉	♍	♒

	1936	1937	1938	1939	1940	1941	1942	1943	1944	1945	1946	1947	1948
JAN	♈	♌	♑	♉	♍	♒	♊	♎	♓	♌	♐	♈	♍
FEB	♉	♎	♒	♊	♏	♈	♌	♐	♉	♍	♑	♊	♎
MAR	♊	♎	♒	♋	♐	♈	♌	♐	♉	♎	♒	♊	♏
APR	♌	♐	♈	♌	♑	♉	♎	♒	♋	♏	[illegible]	♌	♑
MAY	♍	♑	♉	♎	♒	♊	♏	♓	♌	♐	♉	♍	♒
JUN	♎	♒	♋	♏	♈	♌	♑	♉	♎	♒	♊	♏	♐
JUL	♏	♈	♌	♑	♉	♍	♒	♊	♏	♓	♌	♐	♈
AUG	♑	♉	♎	♒	♋	♏	♈	♌	♐	♉	♍	♑	[illegible]
SEP	♓	♋	♏	♈	♌	♑	♉	♍	♒	♋	♏	♓	♌
OCT	♈	♌	♑	♉	♎	♒	♊	♎	♓	♌	♐	♈	♍
NOV	♊	♎	♒	♊	♏	♈	♌	♐	♉	♍	♑	♊	♏
DEC	♋	♏	♓	♌	♑	♉	♍	♑	♊	♎	♒	♋	♐

	1949	1950	1951	1952	1953	1954	1955	1956	1957	1958	1959	1960	1961
JAN	♑	♊	♎	♓	♋	♏	♈	♌	♑	♉	♍	♒	♋
FEB	♓	♋	♐	♈	♍	♑	♉	♎	♒	♊	♏	♈	♌
MAR	♓	♋	♐	♉	♍	♑	♊	♏	♓	♋	♏	♈	♌
APR	♉	♍	♒	♊	♎	♓	♋	♐	♈	♌	♑	♊	♎
MAY	♊	♎	♓	♋	♐	♈	♍	♑	♉	♎	♒	♋	♏
JUN	♌	♐	♈	♍	♑	♊	♎	♓	♋	♐	♈	♌	♑
JUL	♍	♑	♊	♎	♓	♋	♏	♈	♌	♑	♉	♍	♒
AUG	♏	♓	♋	♐	♈	♍	♑	♉	♎	♒	♊	♏	♈
SEP	♐	♈	♍	♑	♊	♎	♒	♋	♐	♈	♌	♑	♊
OCT	♑	♊	♎	♓	♋	♏	♓	♌	♑	♉	♍	♒	♋
NOV	♓	♋	♏	♈	♍	♑	♉	♎	♒	♊	♏	♈	♌
DEC	♈	♌	♑	♊	♎	♒	♊	♏	♓	♌	♐	♉	♍

	1962	1963	1964	1965	1966	1967	1968	1969	1970	1971	1972	1973	1974
JAN	♏	♓	♌	♐	♈	♍	♑	♊	♎	♒	♋	♐	♈
FEB	♐	♉	♍	♒	♊	♏	♓	♋	♏	♈	♍	♑	♉
MAR	♐	♉	♎	♒	♊	♏	♈	♌	♐	♉	♍	♑	♊
APR	♒	♋	♏	♈	♌	♑	♉	♍	♒	♊	♏	♓	♋
MAY	♓	♌	♐	♉	♍	♒	♊	♎	♓	♋	♐	♈	♍
JUN	♉	♎	♒	♊	♏	♓	♌	♐	♉	♍	♑	♊	♎
JUL	♊	♏	♓	♌	♐	♈	♍	♑	♊	♎	♓	♋	♐
AUG	♌	♐	♉	♎	♒	♊	♏	♓	♋	♏	♈	♍	♑
SEP	♍	♒	♋	♏	♓	♋	♐	♉	♍	♑	♊	♎	♓
OCT	♏	♓	♌	♐	♈	♍	♒	♊	♎	♒	♋	♐	♈
NOV	♐	♉	♎	♒	♊	♎	♓	♋	♐	♈	♍	♑	♉
DEC	♑	♊	♏	♓	♋	♐	♈	♌	♑	♉	♎	♒	♊

	1975	1976	1977	1978	1979	1980	1981	1982	1983	1984	1985	1986	1987
JAN	♌	♑	♉	♍	♒	♊	♏	♓	♌	♐	♉	♍	♑
FEB	♎	♒	♋	♏	♈	♌	♐	♉	♍	♒	♊	♎	♓
MAR	♎	♓	♋	♏	♈	♍	♑	♉	♎	♒	♊	♏	♓
APR	♐	♈	♍	♑	♊	♎	♒	♋	♏	♈	♌	♑	♉
MAY	♑	♉	♎	♒	♋	♏	♓	♌	♐	♉	♍	♒	♊
JUN	♓	♋	♐	♈	♌	♑	♉	♎	♒	♊	♏	♓	♌
JUL	♈	♌	♑	♉	♍	♒	♋	♏	♓	♌	♐	♉	♍
AUG	♉	♎	♓	♋	♏	♈	♌	♐	♈	♎	♒	♊	♎
SEP	♋	♐	♈	♌	♐	♊	♎	♒	♊	♏	♓	♌	♐
OCT	♌	♑	♉	♍	♒	♋	♏	♓	♋	♐	♉	♍	♑
NOV	♎	♓	♋	♏	♓	♌	♐	♉	♍	♒	♊	♎	♓
DEC	♏	♈	♌	♐	♉	♍	♑	♊	♎	♓	♋	♐	♈

	1988	1989	1990	1991	1992	1993	1994	1995	1996	1997	1998	1999	2000
JAN	♊	♎	♒	♋	♏	♈	♌	♑	♉	♎	♒	♊	♏
FEB	♋	♐	♈	♍	♑	♉	♎	♒	♋	♏	♈	♌	♐
MAR	♌	♐	♉	♍	♒	♊	♎	♓	♋	♏	♈	♌	♑
APR	♍	♒	♊	♏	♓	♋	♐	♈	♍	♑	♊	♎	♓
MAY	♏	♓	♌	♐	♈	♍	♑	♉	♎	♒	♋	♏	♈
JUN	♐	♉	♍	♑	♊	♎	♓	♋	♐	♈	♌	♑	♉
JUL	♑	♊	♎	♒	♋	♐	♈	♌	♑	♉	♎	♒	♋
AUG	♓	♌	♐	♈	♍	♑	♉	♎	♓	♋	♏	♓	♌
SEP	♉	♍	♑	♊	♏	♓	♋	♏	♈	♌	♑	♉	♎
OCT	♊	♎	♒	♋	♐	♈	♌	♑	♉	♎	♒	♊	♏
NOV	♌	♐	♈	♍	♑	♉	♎	♒	♋	♏	♈	♌	♑
DEC	♍	♑	♉	♎	♒	♋	♏	♈	♌	♐	♉	♍	♒

THE SOLAR SYSTEM

THE STARS, OTHER THAN THE SUN, PLAY NO PART IN THE SCIENCE OF ASTROLOGY. ASTROLOGERS USE ONLY THE BODIES IN THE SOLAR SYSTEM, EXCLUDING THE EARTH, TO CALCULATE HOW OUR LIVES AND PERSONALITIES CHANGE.

Pluto
Pluto takes 246 years to travel around the Sun. It affects our unconscious instincts and urges, gives us strength in difficulty, and perhaps emphasizes any inherent cruel streak.

Neptune
Neptune stays in each sign for 14 years. At best it makes us sensitive and imaginative; at worst it encourages deceit and carelessness, making us worry.

Uranus
The influence of Uranus can make us friendly, kind, eccentric, inventive, and unpredictable.

Saturn
In ancient times, Saturn was the most distant known planet. Its influence can limit our ambition and make us either overly cautious (but practical), or reliable and self-disciplined.

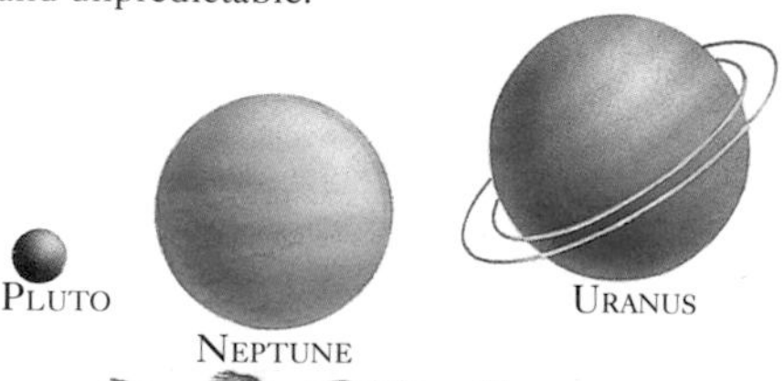

PLUTO

NEPTUNE

URANUS

SATURN

Jupiter

Jupiter encourages expansion, optimism, generosity, and breadth of vision. It can, however, also make us wasteful, extravagant, and conceited.

Mars

Much associated with energy, anger, violence, selfishness, and a strong sex drive, Mars also encourages decisiveness and leadership.

JUPITER

Earth

Every planet contributes to the environment of the Solar System, and a person born on Venus would no doubt be influenced by our own planet in some way.

The Moon

Although it is a satellite of the Earth, the Moon is known in astrology as a planet. It lies about 240,000 miles from the Earth and, sastrologically, is second in importance to the Sun.

MERCURY

THE MOON

VENUS

EARTH

MARS

The Sun

The Sun, the only star used by astrologers, influences the way we present ourselves to the world – our image or personality; the "us" we show to other people.

Venus

The planet of love and partnership, Venus can emphasize all our best personal qualities. It may also encourage us to be lazy, impractical, and too dependent on other people.

Mercury

The planet closest to the Sun affects our intellect. It can make us inquisitive, versatile, argumentative, perceptive, and clever, but maybe also inconsistent, cynical, and sarcastic.